Animal Habitats

The Snake in the Grass

Text by Mike Linley

Photographs by
Oxford Scientific Films

🐌 Belitha Press

Contents

Note: The use of a capital letter for a snake's name indicates that it is a specific *type* of snake (eg North American Garter Snake) and the use of lower case means that it is a member of a larger *group* of snakes.

The Garter Snake is a common species in grasslands near water throughout much of North America.

There are very few snakes that regularly feed on insects.
The Smooth Green Snake eats crickets and spiders.

Snakes in the grass

Snakes are *reptiles*, relatives of lizards, tortoises and crocodiles. Reptiles are cold-blooded animals and rely on the sun to keep warm, so most of them live in the warmer regions of the world. However, snakes can be found in the grasslands of almost every country in the world from Tierra del Fuego, off the Southern tip of South America, to within the Arctic Circle in Northern Europe.

There are around 2,700 *species* of snakes in all, of which less than twenty per cent are *venomous*. Although there are eleven main groups of snakes, more than seventy-five per cent of them belong to one group called the Colubrids. Most of the eleven groups can be found in open *savannah* or grassland. The exceptions are the sea snakes, the river dwelling 'wart' snakes and the desert-living snakes.

In *tropical* regions the temperature is warm and stays more or less the same all year round. There is little difference between winter and summer and the year is divided into 'wet' and 'dry' seasons depending on the rainfall. In tropical grassland, snakes are active all the time. In *temperate* regions, the summers are warm but the winters are often very cold, so the snakes have to *hibernate* for several months to escape the freezing conditions. When spring arrives, the snakes begin to emerge again and warm themselves in the sun.

Rattlesnakes are common on the open prairies of North America. During the day they hunt for small mammals, and at night they hide under rocks and in gopher holes.

Further north, in the wetter grasslands, Garter Snakes hunt for frogs in both the grass and water. In Europe the Grass Snake lives in similar wet grassland areas.

On the hot, dry plains of Africa, Puff Adders and pythons live alongside elephants and gazelles while in Australia, Tiger Snakes and Taipans share their grassland home with kangaroos and rabbits. Strangely enough, there are some large islands, such as Ireland and New Zealand, which have areas of suitable grassy plains, but have no snakes at all. These places have probably remained snake-free, because land snakes rarely enter the sea and so they haven't reached these islands from nearby countries.

Dry grassy plains often catch fire and large numbers of snakes may get killed.

One of the biggest dangers that snakes face on these hot grassy plains, is the threat of fire. In the dry season a fire can sweep through the parched grass quicker than a man can run and many snakes may perish. However, even the shallowest hole may provide a shelter for snakes as the fire frequently burns off only the surface vegetation. The problem is that, when the surviving snakes emerge, they find that they are sitting on a black, charred landscape. The colours that protected them amongst the grass and other plants, now make them stand out against the dead background and leave them open to attack by their many *predators*. But the grass often grows back very quickly and if they can hide until it starts to grow again, then they can usually survive.

In cooler European climates, grassland fires are less common as the ground and the plants are usually too damp. Grassy meadows provide a good *habitat* for frogs and small mammals and so, in turn, a good hunting ground for snakes. But the cold winters mean that it is necessary for the snakes and their *prey* to hibernate.

The Indigo Snake is a large, placid species that feeds on amphibians and small mammals.

Other snakes around the world

Snakes are found everywhere in the world. They thrive in many different kinds of habitat.

Rivers, swamps and marshland are home to a whole variety of snakes. In the Florida Everglades snakes, such as the beautiful Indigo Snake and the venomous Cottonmouth, are very common. Mangrove snakes live among the mud, roots and salty water of the mangrove swamps of South East Asia.

The tropical rain forests of Central and South America, West Africa, Asia and Australia are teeming with snakes that live on the forest floor, under leaves, among tree roots or high up among the branches.

Hot, dry deserts also support large numbers of snakes. In Arizona and Texas snakes are common. Several different types of rattlesnakes and coral snakes, both highly venomous, live amid the sand and cactus plants. Snakes even can live in the vast empty dunes of the Kalahari Desert in South West Africa. The Sidewinding Viper loops its way over the loose sand during the cooler parts of the day. The rest of the time it spends buried with only its nostrils and eyes above the sand. It lies in wait like this, ready to pounce on some passing lizard or small mammal.

Snakes are also found high up in the mountainous regions of the world.

The large eye of the Central American arboreal Parrot Snake is a good indication that it's an active hunter.

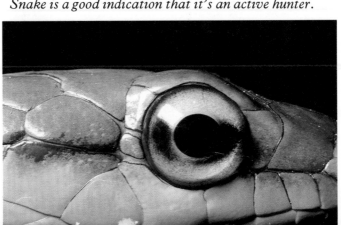

5

The Coral Snake is one of several species whose bodies are brightly coloured to warn that they have a venomous bite.

The snake's body

Snakes vary enormously in size – from the tiny 4-inch (10-cm) burrowing snake to the Reticulated Python of Asia which can reach 32 ft (10 m) in length. The huge South American Anaconda, although not as long as the Reticulated Python, is much heavier – a 29-ft (9-m) specimen might weigh as much as 330 lbs (150 kgs). Anacondas are so heavy that they have to spend much of their time in water to support their enormous weight.

Most people think of a snake as just a head and a long tail. Much of this 'tail' is, in fact, body and the tail itself is quite short. Inside the snake's long, thin body are exactly the same organs as you would expect to find in any other animal except that they, too, are long and thin.

To save space, snakes have only one lung – the right one; the left lung is much smaller and doesn't work.

Snakes are 'cold-blooded' which means that their temperature changes with the temperature of their surroundings. Their internal organs will only work properly above a certain temperature, so snakes have to rely on the sun to keep warm. In tropical regions, the temperature is high enough for snakes to be active all the time but, in cooler countries, snakes must bask in the sun to raise their body temperature.

The snake's body is covered in tough, protective scales, those of the Python are smooth.

Snakes, like all reptiles, are covered with scales. These resemble fish scales and are made of keratin, the same material that makes up our own hair and fingernails. The scales act as a sort of 'armour' that prevents the snake from drying out. In order to grow, a snake has to shed the hard outer layer of its skin occasionally to allow the new, softer scales to grow underneath. Even the *transparent* scale that covers the snake's eye is shed and this turns milky just before the skin is cast. The old skin begins to peel off first around the snake's mouth. Then, as the snake wriggles forward, the whole of the shed skin peels off in one piece, just like someone pulling off a sock.

Although snakes no longer possess legs, they have evolved from lizards which do. There are some primitive snakes, like the boas and pythons, that still have a pair of 'spurs' at the base of the tail. Each spur is, in fact, a single claw, all that remains of the snake's hind limbs which have vanished over millions of years. These spurs are often larger in male snakes and are sometimes used in courtship.

Snakes regularly have to shed their skins in order to grow.

The Tiger Rattler's pit organ lies between its eyes and nostril.

The snake's head

Snakes breathe through a pair of nostrils which are placed just in front of their eyes on the end of the snout. But the nostrils are not used for smelling. Instead, snakes 'taste' the air with their tongues. If you watch a snake carefully, you will see its forked tongue flicks in and out every few minutes, picking up particles of scent in the air or on the ground. The tongue is very sensitive to smells and with it the snake can detect water, food or a mate.

Snakes do not have any ears and they are, in fact, almost deaf. But they do feel vibrations in the ground through the underside of their bodies. They can 'feel' footsteps approaching from many yards (metres) away and, being very shy creatures, they quickly disappear into the undergrowth. This is why you rarely see snakes unless you know where to look for them.

The venomous Gaboon Viper is equipped with some of the longest fangs in the snake world.

8

Snake's eyes differ from species to species. Some snake's eyes have round pupils, others have vertical or horizontal slits, and some snakes have no eyes at all! *Nocturnal* snakes usually have very large eyes, while snakes like the Sidewinding Viper have their eyes placed right on top of their head so that they can see, even when they are buried in the sand. The eyes have no eyelids, but are protected by the transparent scales that cover them.

Between their eyes and nostrils, some snakes have small holes or pits. These are placed either one on each side of the head, or in a row around the upper lip. These 'pit organs' can detect the heat of warm-blooded prey such as rats or mice. So a snake with these pits can find its food, even in complete darkness or down a burrow.

Some snakes are venomous. They have special venom glands in the roof of the mouth and use the venom to kill their prey. They usually inject the poison into their victims through long fangs which act like hypodermic needles. 'Front-fanged' snakes have these hollow teeth at the front of the mouth and 'back-fanged' snakes have them further back. When the snake is ready to strike, it opens its mouth and swings forward its fangs, waiting to give what can be, in many species, a deadly bite.

The Toad-eating Snake from Central America performs a threat display when it is in danger.

Large snakes, like the Python, 'inch' their way forward on their belly scales.

Movement

For animals that have no limbs at all, snakes move in a surprising variety of ways. Snakes of open grassland move across the flat ground in a typical side to side twisting motion, each bend of the snake's body pushing against a rock or clump of grass or against the ground itself. Many snakes use exactly the same 'snaking' movement to swim across or under water. Most snakes take to water readily to hunt for food or escape from danger.

Some of the large, heavy-bodied snakes, such as pythons and puff adders, can move across the ground in a dead straight line. They lift sections of their body off the ground and move forwards as waves of muscular contractions pass along their length. The large scales on the underside of their bodies press against the ground and help to push the snake forward. It's a little like the way a caterpillar or an earthworm moves. When you watch a snake move in this way it becomes obvious that the snake's body is very muscular.

There is another method of *locomotion* used by desert snakes that live on loose sandy dunes where normal forward movement would be impossible. The Sidewinder of South Western USA and the Sidewinding Viper of Namibia have both developed the same method of sideways locomotion even though they are not closely related.

The Sidewinding Viper's curious way of movement leaves curious tracks in the sands of the Namib Desert.

During the rainy season, Cat-eyed Snakes eat large numbers of frog's eggs.

Food and feeding

All snakes are predators, they feed on other animals. There are no snakes that eat plants and, in the wild, most of their prey is caught alive. Snakes are unable to crush, chew or break up their prey. Instead they swallow it whole. So smaller species usually eat small prey and larger species take bigger prey. But even the smallest species can swallow an animal several times the thickness of its own body. A snake is able to do this because the two bones that make up its lower jaw are not joined at the front so each side can move separately. Also both parts of the lower jaw can be unhitched

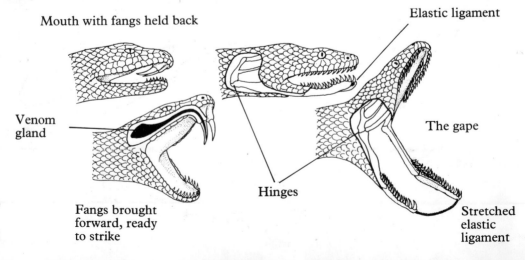

Mouth with fangs held back

Elastic ligament

Venom gland

The gape

Fangs brought forward, ready to strike

Hinges

Stretched elastic ligament

12

at the back from the upper part of the snake's skull. This means that the snake's jaws can be opened very widely. The only thing that limits the size of the snake's *gape* is how much the skin will stretch around its throat. The skin underneath the scales is very elastic and, as the prey is swallowed, the skin stretches and the scales move apart. So a snake with a head the size of a chicken's egg is able to swallow an animal the size of guinea pig!

Although many snakes will eat anything they can swallow, some species specialize in eating a particular type of prey. There are snakes that feed only on bats, or on lizards, or birds, or fish, frogs, frog spawn, crayfish, crickets, snails, slugs, centipedes or termites. There are also many species of snake that feed on other snakes. The non-venomous King Snake of North America gets its name from its habit of overpowering and eating rattlesnakes. Coral Snakes will also eat other snakes, and the huge King Cobra feeds exclusively on other snakes in its native India. But the strangest of all is the African Egg-eating Snake. It feeds only on birds' eggs, even those several times bigger than its own egg. Once an egg has been swallowed whole, special bones inside the snake's throat rub along the egg from side to side. These bones act like a saw and crush the egg. Once the egg is broken, the contents are swallowed. The snake then coughs up the broken shell which is folded up in a neat packet so the edges don't damage its throat.

Egg-eating Snakes feed exclusively on birds' eggs, even large ones many times the diameter of their own body.

Catching prey

Snakes have different ways of catching their prey. Some snakes sit and wait for food while others follow and hunt their prey. The 'sit-and-wait' type are usually *camouflaged* by their colouring to blend in with their background and are not easily seen by their prey. They wait quietly in the grass, ready to strike with lightning speed at any animal that comes within reach. If nothing comes their way, they will move off and try some other suitable place.

Among the hunting snakes there are very few that can actually chase and catch fast-moving prey. Instead they rely on disturbing small animals as they travel through the grass or underground. Some snakes burrow underground in search of small rodents or move under rocks looking for lizards. Many grassland species, such as grass and garter snakes, take to the water in order to hunt for fishes and frogs. Snakes that feed on slow-moving prey such as worms, slugs and snails, simply follow a fresh scent trail until they reach their victims.

Small prey – such as fishes, frogs and earthworms – is normally swallowed alive but larger animals like birds, lizards and mammals have to be killed before being swallowed. Pythons, boas and many other non-venomous snakes kill their prey by *constriction*. They don't crush their prey to death as many people think, they simply wrap their body in several coils around their victim and hold on tightly until the animal dies of *suffocation*.

Even an animal the size of an Impala is easily overpowered and swallowed whole by the African Python.

The King Snake will eat other snakes – even venomous ones.

If a snake comes across a nest of mice or small birds it can constrict several animals at the same time.

Venomous snakes kill their prey by biting and poisoning it. The poison may work in a number of ways. It can cause the victim's blood to clot and so block up veins and arteries, or it can prevent the blood from clotting altogether. Some venoms act upon blood cells and cause them to collapse while others work on the nervous system and cause paralysis and heart failure. Most snakes use a mixture of several types of venom. Generally speaking, a snake's venom is designed to kill its favourite prey. However, snakes will also bite in self-defence, and many species can be dangerous to humans, although they rarely bite people deliberately.

Grass Snakes swallow their prey alive.

Thousands of male Red-sided Garter Snakes wait outside hibernation sites for the females to emerge.

Courtship and mating

Snakes have quite poor eyesight and so don't rely on bright colours, crests or displays to attract a mate. They don't communicate by sound either, in fact, snakes hardly make any noise at all – apart from the odd hiss, or the rattle of a rattlesnake's tail. This isn't surprising when you remember that snakes don't have ears.

Most snakes rely on their sense of smell to track down a mate. The female produces a scent from special glands and from her skin which tells her mate she's in breeding condition. Once a male has tracked her down he moves up and down the length of her body rubbing his chin along her back. The so-called 'mating-dance' of North American rattlesnakes and European vipers isn't a mating dance at all. It is simply a trial of strength between male snakes to establish which is the stronger of the two and therefore, which will mate with a particular female.

The two males wrap around each other like a twisted rope and try and force the other down to the ground. They often push against each other so hard that they spring apart in opposite directions.

Most snakes mate in spring soon after hibernation. The North American Red-sided Garter Snake is one of many species that hibernates throughout the winter. Huge numbers of snakes gather to hibernate in underground chambers. When spring arrives, both males and females are ready to mate. The males emerge from the ground first and hundreds and hundreds of them wait at the entrance to the underground chambers. As the females emerge they are mated immediately by the males. Then they move away into the surrounding grasslands and may not see one another again, until they come together to hibernate in the autumn. In the tropics, where there's little difference between summer and winter, snakes often time their courtship and reproduction with the wet and dry seasons. The wet seasons are usually a good time for producing hatchling snakes as there is often more food available then.

There is one species of snake that doesn't need to find a mate at all. The tiny Flowerpot Snake gets its name from the fact that it's been accidentally transported throughout the warmer regions of the world in the soil of potted plants. Males of this species do not exist, the females simply lay eggs that hatch into more females. So just one animal, arriving in a new warm habitat, can start off a whole new colony. This process of reproduction without males is known as Parthenogenesis.

Red-sided Garter Snakes mating amidst a tangle of other snakes.

*Very few snakes remain with their eggs after they've been laid –
this Corn Snake will abandon its clutch almost immediately.*

Hatching from eggs

Snakes produce their young in one of two ways. Some lay eggs which
hatch out into baby snakes two or three months later. Others keep the
eggs within their bodies and give birth to live, fully-formed young. Some
snakes seem to be half way between the two; they keep their eggs inside
for a while and then lay eggs with well-developed *embryos* that hatch out a
few weeks later.

Snakes' eggs are usually *elongate* with rounded ends. They have a tough
leathery shell, rather than a hard shell like that of a bird's egg. Female
snakes usually lay their eggs in grass tussocks, under logs or under stones
– in fact anywhere that's quite damp and well protected from predators.
The European Grass Snake often chooses piles of rotting vegetation or a
manure heap as a nesting place. The heat given off by the rotting process
helps to *incubate* the eggs. There may be from one to sixty or seventy eggs
laid at any one time.

Once laid, the eggs will soak up water and can start to swell. They can swell to almost double their size before hatching. Once she has laid her eggs, the female snake normally has nothing further to do with them. She leaves the eggs to develop on their own. However, there are a few species that stay and look after their eggs for some time. The Indian King Cobra is said to remain on or close to its nesting place to drive off any likely predators. Many species of python coil around their eggs for up to three months, leaving them only occasionally to go and drink. The Indian Python is also known to twitch frequently while coiled round her eggs. This twitching movement is thought to produce small amounts of heat which warm the eggs and speed up their development.

Inside the eggs, the baby snakes slowly grow and develop. Before hatching, each tiny snake uses an 'egg-tooth' on the end of its snout to pierce and break open the shell. It then struggles out from the egg. Most snake hatchlings remain in the nest area for a few days, until they are ready to shed their skin for the first time. The 'egg-tooth' is shed with the skin – there is obviously no further use for it now. They start to feed within a week of birth and soon become self-sufficient. However, many of the tiny earthworm-sized young snakes will be eaten by predators before they reach maturity, which may take a long as seven years.

Occasionally, twin snakes may emerge from the same egg, but they're often much smaller than normal and very weak. Very rarely 'Siamese' twins may be born, and there are several cases where two-headed snakes have hatched from an egg and survived for many years.

This python's tiny egg-tooth on the end of its snout enables it to rip open its tough egg shell. It will fall off within a week or so.

A hatching snake will often sit for hours with just its head showing before it emerges completely.

Some new born snakes may remain in their thin envelope for an hour or two.

Live young

Many snakes give birth to live, fully-formed young. As the eggs do not need a protective covering inside the mother's body, the shell is replaced by a thin membrane.

There are many advantages in giving birth to live young. Firstly, many animals will eat snake eggs if they can find them, but inside the female's body they're protected. Eggs laid on the ground or under rocks are at the mercy of the weather and in a really cold summer they may not hatch at all. Snakes that live in mountainous regions or in cold climates, like the European Viper that lives inside the Arctic Circle, are live-bearing for exactly this reason. Their eggs would never hatch under such cold conditions. The mother's body also helps to incubate the eggs. She can sit in the sun and bask, raising her body temperature and the temperature of her eggs. The disadvantage of not laying eggs is that the female has to carry

A large, female Garter Snake may give birth to over fifty young at a time.

her eggs inside her for up to three months. This weighs her down and may affect her speed and movement, so that she falls victim to predators more easily.

Carrying eggs around inside its body doesn't necessarily restrict the number of young a snake can produce at one time. The North American Garter Snake may give birth to up to fifty young at a time. In Africa the venomous Gaboon Viper and Puff Adder can have between seventy and a hundred live young. These two species are very heavy-bodied and sluggish in their movement, they rely on their camouflage to escape being seen by predators.

There's a common story among forestry workers of southern Britain, that female adders will swallow their young to protect them if they are disturbed. The story is based on the fact that many adders were killed by foresters as soon as they were sighted. On cutting open the snakes, the men found several live, moving young in what they thought was the snake's stomach. They assumed the snakes had swallowed their young; but the adders were obviously females carrying well-developed eggs, just before they gave birth.

Newly-born rattlers are already fully equipped with venom sacs and fangs.

The African Secretary Bird kills prey by stamping on it with its long, bare legs.

Enemies and defence

Snakes, even venomous species, are eaten by a whole variety of animals including foxes, badgers, weasels and numerous birds of prey. In fact some animals specialize in feeding on snakes. There are even some snakes, like the North American King Snakes that feed entirely on other snakes.

On the grassy plains of Africa, one of the biggest enemies of snakes is the Secretary Bird. This extraordinary bird of prey has enormous long, thin legs that it uses to trample Puff Adders and other deadly snakes to death. It relies on its speed and agility to avoid being bitten. In Spain the Short-toed Eagle specializes in hunting for snakes. It seizes them in its talons and tears at their flesh with its powerful beak. In Europe, hedgehogs regularly kill and eat grass snakes and adders; their sharp spines protecting them from the adder's venomous bite.

The Mongoose's lightning reactions enable it to overpower highly-venomous cobras.

The most famous of all the snake's enemies, however, is the mongoose. Throughout Africa and Asia, mongooses are regularly seen in conflict with cobras – the snake raises its head off the ground, and spreads its hood ready to strike while the little mongoose stands poised, ready to seize the snake by the back of the neck. The mongoose is not totally immune to the cobra's bite, but relies on its quick reactions to avoid being bitten. The mongoose almost always wins.

There are many ways in which a snake can protect itself from enemies. Snakes are very shy creatures; they normally avoid contact with other animals and simply slither away into the undergrowth. Hiding is the best way to escape and any snake exposed on an open grassy plain is in real danger, as it can only move quickly for short distances.

Most snakes can bluff their way out of danger by putting on a display – either by spreading a hood, inflating the neck or gaping the mouth. These displays, accompanied by loud hissing, usually frighten off most predators. The European Grass Snake and American Hog-nosed Snake roll over onto their backs and pretend to be dead when threatened. This may help to save them, since many predators are not interested in what they think is dead food.

Many snakes, when alarmed can produce a foul-smelling liquid from special glands in their bodies. This is often enough to put an attacker off. If you handle one of these snakes, the smell remains on your hands and clothes for days and days. The Spitting Cobra can actually spray its venom into the eyes of predators, causing them intense pain and even blindness, while the snake makes its escape.

The Grass Snake pretends to be dead when danger threatens in the hope that the predator will leave it alone.

The Copperhead is well camouflaged among dried leaves.

Camouflage, warning colours and mimicry

One of the best forms of defence is to try and avoid being seen altogether. Most snakes have colours and markings which allow them to blend in with their surroundings. This is called camouflage. As well as helping them to escape from enemies, camouflage also enables a snake to sneak up on prey, such as lizards, without being seen.

On a plain background the Puff Adder is easily seen, its bright colours and markings stand out. But on a background of dead grass the snake merges into its background so well that it completely disappears, even though it can be over 5 feet (1.5 m) in length and is thicker than a man's arm.

Many snakes go out of their way to be seen. This is the opposite of camouflage. The deadly coral snakes warn other animals that they are venomous by being coloured in bands of red, yellow and black. These warning colours also serve to startle attackers when the snake is disturbed from under a rock or pile of dead leaves. There are also some harmless species, including some king and milk snakes, that are coloured in exactly the same way as coral snakes. Their colouring is designed to fool predators who will think they have a poisonous bite and leave them alone. These brightly-coloured reptiles are among the world's most beautiful snakes.

Grass Snakes are almost invisible when they sit motionless in a tussock.

This copying by a non-venomous animal of the colours of a venomous one is common throughout nature and is known as *mimicry*, because one species mimics the other.

There are also some snakes which are generally well camouflaged but, when disturbed, can 'flash' bright colours at an intruder to startle it and scare it away. The American Ringneck Snake has bright red scales on the underside of its tail which it lifts up in the air when alarmed. The display often works quite well, and frightens away predators even though the Ringneck Snake is only a foot (30 cm) long!

Many other snakes mimic the vivid colours of the coral snake to fool predators.

Rattlesnakes vibrate their rattles so that large animals such as bison hear them and avoid treading on them.

Friends and neighbours

As you might imagine, snakes have few friends on the grassy plains and savannahs of the world. Most other animals are usually either small enough to be eaten by the snake or large enough to pose a threat to it. There are some animals, though, that can live side by side with snakes.

In North America, the Prairie Rattlesnake once shared the open plains with vast herds of buffalo. The only threat to the snakes was when a buffalo accidentally trod on one. This is probably the reason why the rattlesnake has a rattle on the end of its tail, to warn large herd animals of its presence and prevent it being squashed. The 'rattle' is made up of loose single scales that rattle against each other when the snake shakes its tail. The rattler starts off life with one tiny button of a scale but, each time

The North American prairies are home to a large number of snakes as well as large animals like the bison.

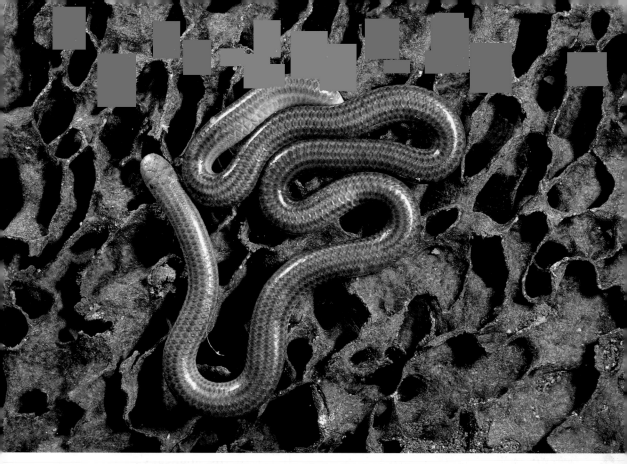

The tiny Blind Snake spends its life in termite mounds.

the snake sheds its skin, this end scale is kept and rattles against the new one, to make a full set of noisy rattling scales.

Gopher snakes in the same region sometimes live in the warren of burrows made by gophers and may even eat young gophers. But they also share this home with other animals, such as the gopher tortoise and gopher frog, both of which use the burrows as a retreat. In the vast, open, grassy plains, gopher holes or the burrows of Ground Squirrels are, very often, the only places where animals can hide.

On the vast plains of Africa many species of snake live alongside huge herds of game animals. Puff Adders and egg-eating snakes share their home with zebra, giraffe, antelope and even elephants and hippos.

European Grass Snakes usually live close to water and feed almost entirely on fish and *amphibians*. They may often hide under the same rock or fallen log as a common lizard or another snake such as the adder. Some snakes lay their eggs inside termite mounds where the warm, damp atmosphere provides ideal conditions for their incubation. This does not seem to upset the termites too much.

There's even a snake in East and Southern Africa, called the House Snake that lives in the roofs or foundations of houses. It is of great value to the human residents by ridding their houses of mice and rats.

27

Goorialla, the giant Rainbow Serpent from the beginning of the Dreamtime, painted by Dick Roughsey, one of Australia's most famous Aborigine artists.

Snakes and people

Because people can be poisoned or killed by venomous snakes, they are often feared and hated more than any other animals. There are many people throughout the world whose first reaction on seeing a snake is to kill it, whether it is venomous or not. Some people even have unreasonable fears about snakes and are greatly affected when they see one, even if it's just in a photograph.

Throughout history, snakes have had a powerful effect on human beings. Some civilizations looked upon snakes as gods and worshipped them. To the early Australian Aborigines snakes were rain gods, while in ancient Egypt, they were a symbol of fertility. Nowadays more people fear snakes than worship them.

Snakes can be very dangerous and in some countries many people die from snake bites. In India alone it has been estimated that the total number of deaths from snakebite each year is between 10,000 and 12,000. Throughout South East Asia the story is very similar. In India the deadly snakes are usually cobras and vipers. In fact, the Saw-scaled Viper, in terms of human deaths, is the world's most dangerous snake, killing over 20,000 people every year.

Most people die from snake bite because of the lack of medical help nearby. Many more people would recover from snake bites if they were treated quickly enough. In the United States, where there are many cases of rattlesnake bite, the number of people who die each year is less than 15 because suitable treatment is readily available.

Snakes can also be useful to people. They are eaten by many people especially the Chinese and in China and Hong Kong shops full of live and dead snakes are common. Snake-skin is also used throughout the world for making shoes, handbags and belts. But many of the species used are now in danger of becoming extinct, so some countries have restricted the import of snake skins.

In North Africa and India snake-charmers have entertained foreigners for centuries. Their snakes, usually cobras, appear out of baskets and sway, as though hypnotised, to the music of the charmer's pipe. Because snakes are almost deaf and cannot hear the music, it's the shape and swaying movement of the pipe that attracts them.

Snake charmers are popular tourist attractions in North Africa and India.

Life in the grass

Grasslands vary throughout the world, but generally speaking, they provide a good *environment* for snakes. In tropical regions the grasslands are often teeming with life – a limitless supply of food. The only thing that varies in these areas is the amount of rainfall. In a good year the small mammals and lizards breed well and so do the predatory snakes, but in a bad year when there's little food available, the snakes suffer too, although snakes can go for a surprisingly long time – certainly many months – without food. In their grassland environment snakes are both the predators of smaller animals and the prey of larger ones. They, thus, are an important part of the grassland food chain.

Food chain

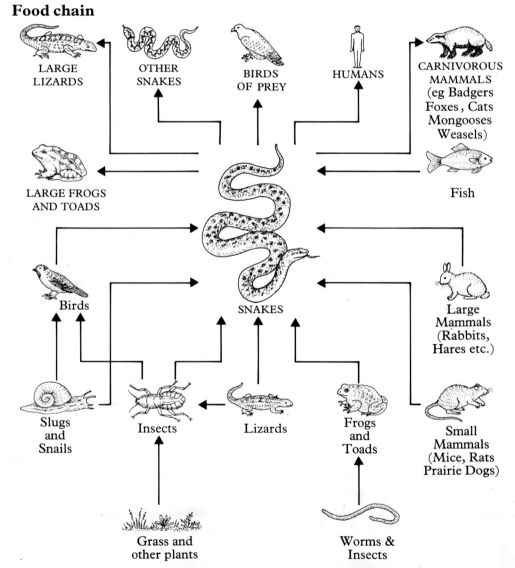

LARGE LIZARDS

OTHER SNAKES

BIRDS OF PREY

HUMANS

CARNIVOROUS MAMMALS (eg Badgers Foxes, Cats Mongooses Weasels)

LARGE FROGS AND TOADS

Fish

Birds

SNAKES

Large Mammals (Rabbits, Hares etc.)

Slugs and Snails

Insects

Lizards

Frogs and Toads

Small Mammals (Mice, Rats Prairie Dogs)

Grass and other plants

Worms & Insects

In Europe the Grass Snake is the most common grassland species.

Grassland habitats are obviously very important for the lives of many snakes. Unfortunately, the biggest threat to these environments comes from humans. In temperate countries, rich meadows are usually a good place to farm crops and, as a result, they are often ploughed up and cultivated. Many other grassland areas are turned over to building land. Snakes can survive around the edges of fields, provided there's plenty of cover and the farmer does not use too many chemicals. But snakes do not survive well in gardens. Snakes are shy and wary creatures and avoid contact with humans if at all possible. If a snake is left alone and not molested it will quickly slide away through the grass without harming anyone. If you are lucky enough to see a snake in the wild, keep still and watch it move away. It's far more frightened of you than you are of it.

31

Glossary

amphibians: animals such as frogs, toads, newts, which can live both on land and in water 5, 27

camouflage: animal disguise – the way in which an animal hides by blending in with its background 14, 21, 24, 25

constriction: squeezing prey tightly to cause death by suffocation 14

elongate: a long, tapered oval-shape 18

embryo: the developing animal inside the egg 18

environment: the natural surroundings 30, 31

gape: the width of the widely opened mouth of a vertebrate animal 12, 13

habitat: the natural home of any plant or animal 4, 5, 17, 31

hibernate: to sleep over winter 3, 4, 17

locomotion: the act or power of movement 11

mimicry: the resemblance shown by one animal species to another which protects it from predators 24, 25

nocturnal: active only at night 9

predator: an animal that kills and eats other animals 4, 12, 18, 19, 21, 23, 24, 25, 30

prey: an animal that is hunted by anothe animal for food 4, 9, 12, 13, 14, 1! 22, 24

reptiles: a group of animals, including lizards, snakes, crocodiles and tortoises, which are cold-blooded and covered in horny scales 3, 7

savannah: flat, open grassland with occasional trees 3

species: a type of animal (or plant) which can interbreed successfully with others of its kind, but not with those of a different type 2, 3, 5, 6, 12, 13, 14, 15, 17, 19, 21, 25, 27, 3!

suffocation: blockage of oxygen to the air passages causing discomfort and death 14

temperate: the cooler regions of the earth between the tropics and the poles 3, 31

transparent: clear enough to see through 7

tropical: relating to the hot areas around
(tropics) the middle of the earth to the nort! and south of the equator 3, 5, 6

venomous: referring to an animal, such as a snake, scorpion or spider which secretes poisonous fluid 3, 5, 6, 8, 9, 13, 14, 15, 21, 22, 24, 25

The line drawings are by Lorna Turpin.

First published in Great Britain 1990
by Belitha Press Ltd
31 Newington Green, London N16 9PU
Text © Oxford Scientific Films 1990
Consultant Editor: Jennifer Coldrey
Art Director: Treld Bicknell   Design: Naomi Games
ISBN 0 947553 62 2
Printed in the United States

The author and publishers wish to thank the following for permission to reproduce copyright material: **Oxford Scientific Films Ltd.** for title page, pp 6, 9, 12 and 13 *both* (M. P. L. Fogden); pp 24, 25 *below* and back cover (Animals Animals – Zig Leszczynski); pp 7 *above*, 19 *both* and 23 (G. I. Bernard); pp 24, 25 *below* and back cover (Animals Animals – Breck Kent); pp 2 and 26 *above* (Leonard Lee Rue); p 14 and front cover (Stan Osolinski); pp 16 and 17 (Animals Animals – Brian Milne); pp 20 *above* and 21 (Tony & Sheila Phelps); p 3 (Animals Animals – Lynn M. Stone); p 4 (David Cayless); p 5 *below* (Philip Sharpe); p 8 *above* (Stephen Dalton); p 8 *below* (Michael Dick); p 10 (C. W. Helliwell); p 11 (Anthony Bannister); p 15 *below* (Avril Ramage); p 20 *below* (Animals Animals – Joe McDonald); p 22 *above* (P. & W. Ward); p 22 *below* (Animals Animals – E. R. Degginger); p 25 *above* (Barrie E. Watts); p 26 *below* (Tom Ulrich); p 27 (Gerald Thompson); p 29 (Robert M. Kloepper). Collins Publishers Australia for p 28 *The Rainbow Serpent* by Dick Roughsey.